*Play*

L

*Play the Game*

# Rugby League

John Huxley

WARD LOCK

**Half-title page:** *Jason Robinson dives at the corner to score for England during the 1995 World Cup match against Australia*

**Title page:** *The Castleford squad demonstrate excellent coordinated defence in successfully tackling Chris McKinney of Oldham and pulling him to the ground*

**Above:** *Despite determined resistance from players such as Bradford's Nathan Graham, St Helen's went on to win the 1996 Silk Cut Challenge Cup Final by 40 points to 32*

# Contents

# Foreword

**During the last few years Rugby League has developed into one of the world's most exciting and demanding team sports. It is now not only a super spectacle for the paying spectator but also an even more incredible game to play.**

The future of Rugby League depends on the number of youngsters we attract to play the game. It is therefore very pleasing to see *Play the Game: Rugby League* has been updated to meet the requirements of the modern game.

At professional level we expect our players to be fitter and more highly skilled than ever before. It is vital that players, coaches and administrators, at all levels of both the amateur and professional game, possess the necessary skills to carry out their duties effectively to ensure that the game continues to go from strength to strength.

During the past few years Rugby League in Britain has experienced a period of rapid change. It is of great importance that the people who spend time with our young players are kept as up to date as possible with all changes occurring within the game. This book will be the ideal aid to those leaders as they pass on the spirit and traditions of the game of Rugby League as well as the skills. We are all striving to ensure that Rugby League is played in a safe environment, which will enable players and spectators alike to gain maximum enjoyment from the game.

Finally Rugby League is now played by both boys and girls and men and women. We are always conscious of the need to provide everyone with the very best of coaching help and information. Rugby League is a competitive and demanding game to play and I applaud Ward Lock's decision to put the game where it belongs, on a par with the rest of the major sports of the world, by including it in the *Play the Game* series.

**Maurice P. Lindsay**
*Chief Executive of the*
*Rugby Football League*

The British Amateur Rugby League Association has been described by the Sports Council as one of British sport's greatest success stories over the last decade, and not without just cause. Association membership has increased by more than 1300 teams and many in the crucial area of Youth Rugby.

Leagues and clubs are now established and prospering in the Midlands and London, as well as in the north-east of England. The student game is also much expanded to more than sixty teams in the various Student Leagues.

A game which was once very parochial is also extending its international boundaries and foreign tours are now the order of the day. Indeed, since BARLA's formation in 1973, there have been as many as thirty tours to and from the Southern Hemisphere, with pioneer visits to Western Samoa, Fiji, South Africa and Tonga.

Rugby League has also established its own very successful Rugby League National Coaching Scheme.

The aim of BARLA is to maximize the base of grassroots involvement in Rugby League football and we are sure that this excellent publication will play an important role in helping us achieve that objective.

**Maurice F. Oldroyd**
*Chief Executive of the*
*British Amateur Rugby League Association*

# History & development of Rugby League

**While the origins of football are lost in the mists of time, Rugby League can proudly point to its birthday: 29 August 1895.**

The date marks the second of two important breakaways from primitive football, which in England in the early nineteenth century was played according to various sets of rules and was usually a scrimmaging, kicking and mauling game in which two teams of players tried to force the ball into their opponents' goal or across an agreed boundary line.

At Rugby School the boys played a non-handling version of the game, and the first break with tradition occurred in 1823 when a pupil called William Webb Ellis picked up the ball and ran with it. Two codes of football then began to evolve: in the Rugby version, the players handled and ran with an oval ball; in the other version, now known as soccer, they kicked a round ball.

The English Rugby Football Union was formed in 1871, and by 1893 had attracted some 400 member clubs. By then, however, a North–South divide was making itself felt. The Rugby Football

Union held fast to its belief in the spirit of amateurism, but the harsh reality of life in the industrial north of England made it difficult to adhere to that code and make a living at the same time.

In those days men used to work in mills, mines and factories all through Saturday to make a living wage for themselves and their families. If they took Saturday afternoon off to play Rugby football they lost money and their families suffered. To encourage them to take time off work some clubs wanted to pay what was known as 'broken time'. The argument was that they were not paying wages, which was strictly against the amateur principle, but giving compensation for missing a valuable shift at work.

The rulers of the Union game were afraid that if they gave in to the Northern clubs on the issue of broken time, they would be opening the door to professionalism. Pressure for change built up in the North and, on 20 September 1893, the inevitable clash between the two factions took place at the Rugby Union's annual meeting in London.

Two Yorkshire club representatives, Mr J. A. Millar and Mr M. Newsome, proposed: 'Players are to be allowed compensation for bona-fide loss of time.' The motion was lost by 418 votes to 136, but there was enough support to create a body of clubs who met regularly to discuss their predicament. Sufficient progress was made to call a meeting of Northern clubs at the George Hotel, Huddersfield on 29 August 1895 to discuss the situation.

Only one of the representatives, the gentleman from Dewsbury, voted against the proposition that the clubs resign from the Rugby Union and form their own Northern Rugby Union and so be able legally to pay their players broken-time expenses. Once it became known that the split had been made, two more clubs, Stockport and Runcorn, joined the breakaway band. A period of furious work followed but, by Saturday 7 September 1895, the new code was ready with its first set of fixtures.

Retribution was not long in coming. The Rugby Union forbade its member clubs to play against any from the Northern Union, and introduced even stricter rules against payments to players. The Northern Union, out on their own, began to develop their game. Broken-time rates were set at six shillings (30p) and several of the wealthier clubs set a pattern for the future by paying their better players slightly more than the basic rate. By the first annual meeting in 1896, the Northern Union had 59 member teams. Among the new arrivals the following season were present-day League members Bramley, Castleford, Salford and Swinton.

The next major event was the introduction of the Northern Union Cup, the forerunner of today's Challenge Cup. It was a knock-out competition and the first final, in 1897, was played before a crowd of almost 14,000. At this stage the Northern Union was still playing under Rugby Union laws but, at the end of the second season, the first signs of a real split appeared.

To make the Northern Union game more attractive to specta-tors, it was decided to make various changes. The points value for scoring was altered so that every type of goal counted as two points and the line-out was eliminated. These changes were followed in 1906 by one of the main features that separates Rugby League from the Union game: the reduction to thirteen men a side – a move designed to open up the game by cutting down on the number of forwards. The idea was an immediate success and another distinguishing feature was then introduced: after each completed tackle there would be a two-man scrum or play-the-ball.

After the second Challenge Cup, in 1898, the players noting the huge attendance of 27,941 called for the abolition of broken-time expenses and the introduction of full professionalism. Their argument was accepted by the 1898 annual meeting and profes-sional players have been a fundamental part of the senior section of the game ever since. With money being paid openly, the creation of more successful teams became important and the search for top players moved outside the north into Rugby Union strongholds such as south Wales, the south-west and north-east of England.

Until 1900 the Northern Rugby Union ran two county leagues, one each in Lancashire and Yorkshire, and the Challenge Cup. In 1901 the first combined league of the game's top clubs was brought into operation with twelve clubs: Batley, Bradford, Broughton Rangers, Halifax, Huddersfield, Hull, Hunslet, Oldham, Runcorn, Salford, Swinton and Warrington. The competition was called the Northern Rugby League. Later it was agreed to take the winners of a play-off between the winners of the county competitions into the new league each season, giving the Northern Union an early form of promotion and relegation. Such was the success of the 'super league' that attendances at the county games fell and this led to a fall in the number of clubs the following season.

Again the Northern RU was forced to adapt and, for season 1902–03, it was decided to introduce a two-division system with a first and second section each of eighteen clubs. This did not last long and in 1905 one large league was created.

It was not long before the new Northern Union code became attractive to other Rugby-playing nations. During the 1905 New Zealand All Black tour to Britain a member of their party, winger George W. Smith, met Northern Union officials and players. He was so impressed that he agreed to recruit a party of New Zealand players to tour Britain playing as professionals.

Back home Smith and another enthusiast, Albert Henry Baskerville, succeeded in collecting enough players to mount a tour to Great Britain in 1907–08. While they were making the arrangements for the trip they received a cable from a group of Australians interested in their scheme. They agreed to play three exhibition games under Union laws in Australia on their way to Britain, and recruited top Australian player Herbert Henry 'Daily' Messenger in consequence. They had also acquired a nickname, the 'All Golds', bestowed on them by fellow New Zealanders who disapproved of them leaving the Union ranks and being paid for playing Rugby.

The tourists arrived in Britain in October 1907. After initial success at Bramley and Huddersfield, a series of defeats followed. The news that they had been suspended for life by the New Zealand Union did little to lift the tourists' spirits and in the historic first Northern Union Test at Headingley on 25 January 1908 they were defeated 14–6.

The result might have been predictable but the British sporting public were still curious about this new-style touring team and, for the second Test at Chelsea's Stamford Bridge ground in London, 15,000 turned up to watch as the All Golds levelled the series with an 18–6 victory. The scene switched to Cheltenham and the deciding Test, which went to the Australasian tourists 8–5.

As in modern Rugby League, the touring players who did well became targets for success-hungry British clubs. Winger George Smith signed for Oldham and one of the most popular players, half-back Lance Todd, who was later to have an important role in the game's development as an administrator and journalist, joined Wigan. The returning All Golds played three games in Australia on the way home, this time under Northern Union laws. This encouraged the New South Wales Rugby Union to break away and form their own Rugby League and adopt the Northern Union laws.

The game was now in place in Australia and that proved to be a major breakthrough for the new code. In 1908, a year after the New Zealanders, the first Australian touring team sailed for Britain. Today's intense Test match rivalry between the two countries had its beginnings at Queen's Park Rangers ground in London. The result was a thrilling 22–22 draw, although the crowd of 2,000 was disappointing. For the second Test the Northern Union continued its policy of staging its big matches at 'propaganda' centres, in an attempt to spread the game. This time, at St James' Park, Newcastle-upon-Tyne, there were 22,000 spectators and they saw the Northern Union win 15–5. The crunch Third Test was played at Villa Park, Birmingham and, although the British won the match and the series, a very disappointing attendance made the event an anti-climax. At the end of the tour a number of players decided to stay, including winger Albert Rosenfeld who joined Huddersfield. In 1913–14 he scored 80 tries in the season – a record that still stands.

While the game was spreading overseas, the Northern Union was still trying to break out of its main stronghold and in 1908 Barry, Aberdare, mid-Rhondda and Treherbert were admitted to join two other Welsh clubs, Ebbw Vale and Merthyr Tydfil.

After receiving two sets of tourists, the Northern Union ventured out of the UK for the first time in 1910 and travelled to Australia and New Zealand. For the first Test on Australian soil there was a fantastic 42,000 crowd in Sydney and the British won 27–20. The two met again in Brisbane and again the British tourists came out on top, 22–17. The Australians, however, have never recognized this match as an official Test; although they played several New Zealanders in their teams for two later matches, one of which they won and the other they drew, they preferred to include these matches in their official records.

The new code of Rugby League was established. Virtually all connections with its Union parentage had gone, apart from those individual players who crossed British sport's greatest divide. Competition was suspended from 1915 until 1919 because of the First World War, then there followed a major boom in Northern Union's popularity as a spectator sport.

*Good ball handling skills are of paramount importance when resisting a coordinated tackle*

Three years later the game chose its modern identity. Delegates at the 1922 annual meeting decided to ditch the localized name of Northern Union and adopt a new all-embracing label of Rugby Football League. In 1927 the Challenge Cup final, Oldham v Swinton at Wigan, was broadcast for the first time on radio. Two years later, following much argument, came a major change in policy: the Cup final moved to London and its spiritual home, Wembley. The first Wembley final was between mighty Wigan and little Dewsbury from West Yorkshire. Wigan won 13–2, and the big crowd of 41,500 vindicated the decision to move the game south. Now Rugby League Cup final day is a traditional high spot on the British sporting calendar.

The French and Rugby go naturally together, especially in the south-west of their country. In 1933, at a time when the French were suspended from the international Union game on charges of professionalism, they sent a delegation to meet English League officials. As a direct result of those talks the 1933–34 Australian tourists played an exhibition game against Great Britain at Stade Pershing in Paris. There was a crowd of 20,000 and they saw the Kangaroos win 63–13 on a frozen pitch.

The French had acquired the taste for Rugby League and, led by Jean Galia, a former French Union international, a number of other players were persuaded to switch codes and tour Britain. They won just one of their matches but they were inspired to develop the game in their country. In April 1934 the Fédération Française de Jeu à Treize (game for thirteen) was launched and in 1935 a European championship with England and Wales was created.

Since their admission to the code the French had been pushing hard for a World Cup competition. After the Second World War they at last got their wish and staged the first-ever tournament in 1954; much to everyone's surprise, a weakened British team led by a former Scots Rugby Union player Dave Valentine were the winners! In recognition of their contribution to the sport, games against the French were elevated to Test-match status in 1957.

In the post-war sports boom in Britain, Rugby League was still trying to expand outside its north of England heartland. In 1952 the Challenge Cup final was televised nationally for the first time.

The League decided to try a two-division format again for 1962–63, but the experiment lasted just two seasons; Swinton won the championship each time. In 1964 substitutes were allowed for the first time. They could be used to replace injured players, but only until half-time. A year later the League gave the go-ahead for replacement players to be allowed for any reason up to and including the interval. The same year, 1965, the English Schools Rugby League was formed.

For some years Rugby League had been seeking ways to make itself more attractive to spectators. It was felt that the law allowing one team to hold possession for as long as it could was detracting from the spectacle. So, in 1966, a limit of four successive tackles was imposed. After a team had reached that limit they either had to kick the ball or concede possession to a scrummage. In 1972 the limit was extended to six tackles.

Another major change was to play matches on a Sunday. The experiment was started in 1967 and soon Sunday became the normal match-day for the professional code. In 1969 substitutes were allowed at any stage in the match, and Universities Rugby League was introduced. In 1971 the prestigious John Player competition was launched, and the following year match time-keeping was taken away from the referees and handed over to two club officials, one from each side, who signalled half-time and the end of a match with a hooter.

A third attempt to make two divisions work was started in 1973, and this time the League, despite constant opposition from some clubs, have stayed with the system. Amateur Rugby League had reached a major crisis point, however. The number of leagues and clubs had fallen so dramatically that the grass-roots game virtually died. Alarmed by this situation a group of enthusiasts met in Huddersfield to form the British Amateur Rugby League Association (BARLA), which took control of that side of the game.

A new end-of-season competition, the Premiership, was launched in 1975. Until 1996 the top eight clubs faced each other in this knock-out competition after the end of the League competition. The top four took home venues then the other four were drawn against them. The system was introduced to the second division in 1987 and was then adapted so that clubs in the second and third division competed in one competition, playing their final on the same day as the top-division clubs. In 1997 the twelve Super League clubs were all included in one competition.

In 1978 the game expanded internationally for the first time since the French were admitted in the 1930s when Papua New Guinea were granted full international board status. The game had been taken there by Australian servicemen in the Second World War and it has become their national sport.

A controversial development in 1983 was the sin bin. Under this system players can be sent off for spells of ten minutes and then can return to the action. British Rugby League took some time to come to terms with the sin bin, although Australia and New Zealand, who suggested the idea, adapted to the system very quickly. In the same year the value of the try was up-rated from three to four points and a new law was introduced making players hand the ball over if they still had it after six completed, successive tackles. In 1988 a further change came in, designed to speed up the game still further. Australian-inspired, it forced players in possession after five tackles to keep the ball in play rather than end the action.

The shape of the professional game in Britain was changed dramatically in April 1995 when it was agreed to join Super League, a new Rugby League organization funded by media corporation multi-millionaire Rupert Murdoch and founded in Australia. The British game was given an exclusive contract by the new organization for five years, which brought an incredible £87 million into the professional sport and saw it broadcast on satellite television.

Just as revolutionary was the decision to change the playing season from the winter-dominated sector of August to May to the summer-led March to October–November period. This decision, which was implemented from 1996, brought the European game in line with its Australasian counterpart.

The European Super League introduced a French team, Paris St Germain, for the first time in 1996 and they joined eleven British clubs in the top competition while the rest of the British game was divided into a first and second division, both of eleven clubs.

In Britain there are approximately 1,750 professional players with around 25,000 amateur players who regularly play the game for fun. Since 1995 Super League players are, in general, full-time professional players while in the first and second divisions the players are mostly part-time professionals. That means that they have other jobs but are paid by clubs for training and playing.

Super League clubs play each other on a home-and-away basis

to decide the championship while the first and second divisions operate on the same basis. First division clubs can gain promotion by winning their league title, although there are plans to introduce new clubs on a franchise basis for 1998. The winner is promoted to Super League while the bottom club in Super League is relegated to the first division. The bottom two clubs in the first division drop into the second division while the top two clubs in the second division are promoted. Again the League was planning more changes for 1998 and these include possible League format alterations. Outside the professional game the top amateurs play in the National Amateur League while a Conference has been formed for players outside the north of England.

The top Leagues in the world are not in Britain but Australia. When Super League was first announced in 1995 it split the Australian game in half. One set of clubs and players gave their loyalty to Super League and the other stayed with the original governing body, the Australian Rugby League. The ten-club Australian Super League kicked off in 1997 playing alongside the ten-club Australian Rugby League tournament, although there are now plans for the two competitions to be amalgamated following peace talks.

In Australia Rugby League is the premier sport in New South Wales and Queensland and is played to a lesser extent in the continent's other states. New clubs have been formed in Adelaide and Melbourne.

In New Zealand the sport has developed rapidly since the Auckland Warriors were introduced into the Australian game and now play in the Super League. There are approximately sixteen leagues in New Zealand with the Lion Red competition being the most senior. Most of the players in New Zealand play as amateurs although many of them have been signed to play for British and Australian clubs as professionals. French Rugby League has suffered a decline in the last two decades. Their Federation of clubs is based in the south-west of the country where they play on a part-time professional basis. There are a number of amateur clubs in the Paris region while the top club in the country is Paris St Germain, which uses French players together with a series of imported stars from Australia. Paris St Germain played in Super League in 1996 and 1997 but was closed for 1998 pending a re-opening in 1999.

# Equipment & terminology

Most Leagues and competitions define the minimum size of pitch acceptable to them; smaller pitches may be laid out for schoolboy games.

### The pitch

Rugby League is played on a grass surface. The pitch is rectangular and must not be longer than 100m (109yd) and 68m (74yd) wide. The in-goal areas at either end of the pitch may vary in depth from 6–11m (6–11yd).

The boundary lines down the 'long' side of the pitch are called touch-lines and those joining the outer corners of the in-goal areas are the dead-ball lines.

The modern Rugby League pitch closely resembles an American Football playing surface with grid-iron-style markings which assist players and match officials during the game. It also provides spectators with a guide as to the progress or otherwise of their side during any one play.

The three most important lines marked on the pitch are those at halfway and 20m (68ft). They divide the pitch into 'quarters' which often have a major bearing on the tactical approach employed by teams during the match.

touch

max.100m (109yd)

touch-line

10m (34ft)

10m (34ft)

halfway line

in-goal area

goal-line

20m line

centre spot

20m line

goal-line

In-goal area

dead-ball line

dead-ball line

max. 68m (75yd)

6–11m (19–37ft)

10m (34ft)

touch in-goal

10m (34ft)

touch-line

touch in-goal

10 20 30 40 50 40 30 20 10

touch

THE RUGBY LEAGUE PITCH

In the middle of the halfway line is the centre spot from which is taken the kick-off to start the game or to re-start it following a score. The rest of the pitch is marked out in 10m (34ft) segments. A broken line runs parallel with the touch-line – the line down the outside of the pitch – and a further line runs parallel with these two lines 20m (68ft) in from the touch-line, showing where scrummages are to be positioned for the re-start of the match after a successful kick for touch. The scrummage is staged at the point where the ball crossed the touch-line.

The area where the match takes play is known as the 'field of play' and at either end of this area is a box called the in-goal area. This is where a player attempts to place the ball down for a try. The start of the in-goal area is marked with the goal-line and the end of it is indicated by the dead-ball line.

THE RUGBY LEAGUE BALL

circumference
58–61cm
(22³/₄–24in)

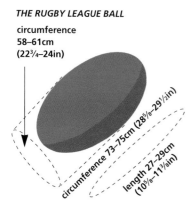

weight 380–440g (13²/₅–15¹/₂oz)

THE RUGBY LEAGUE GOAL-POSTS

crossbar

min. 4m (13.1ft)

3m (10ft)

5.5m (18ft)

protective padding

For Super League games the pitches tend to be marked in bold colours and the end quarters have been experimentally designated 'red zones', so that television audiences and spectators can see that attacking players are approaching the goal-line and defending players are in a critical position. Numbers on the pitch indicating each 10m (34ft) zone were used for the World Cup Championship in 1997 and may be officially adopted in the future.

## The ball

Rugby League, like Rugby Union, is played with an oval-shaped ball. The outer casing should be made of leather or a similar material which can be inflated. It should weigh, when dry and clean, 380–440g (13²/₅–15¹/₂oz) and measure 58–61cm (22³/₄–24in) at its widest circumference, 27–29cm (10⁵/₈–11³/₈in) in length and 73–75cm (28⁵/₈–29¹/₂in) at its longest circumference. If the ball deflates during the game the referee has to stop the game and swap it for another.

## The goal-posts

One of the most distinctive features of any Rugby pitch is the pair of H-shaped goal-posts. There are strict rules governing their shape and size. They consist of two upright posts joined together by a crossbar, and are positioned on the goal-line at an equal distance from each touch-line. A goal may be scored when the ball goes through the uprights above the crossbar; to help the officials decide whether the ball has passed through the posts correctly, the uprights are considered to extend indefinitely upwards.

The uprights, which may be made of wood or tubular metal, must be more than 4m (13.1ft) high and 5.5m (18ft) apart with the crossbar a minimum of 3m (10ft) off the ground.

## The flag-posts

Flag-posts are placed at the junction of the goal-lines and touch-lines. Made of a non-rigid material, they should not be more than 1.25m (4ft) high.

## Players' equipment

All players in a team must wear the same colour of jersey, socks and shorts. The jerseys are usually numbered to indicate the players' positions. If there is a clash in the teams' colours the referee can

*This is how a Rugby League player dresses for the game*

instruct either team to change to an alternative, distinctive strip; generally, it is the away team which has to change colours. Shoulder or body protection pads are allowed as long as they do not contain any rigid materials, and quite a number of modern professionals use head-guards or strips of tape to protect their ears.

On their feet players wear the type of boot which suits their position on the field. Most forwards choose a high-sided boot which provides support for the ankle, while most back-division players prefer a lighter, shoe-type boot. Studs in the sole of the boot are permitted but they must not have a diameter of more than 8mm ($^5/_{16}$in) at the apex and if metal the studs must have rounded edges. They may vary in length to suit the pitch conditions but they must not be dangerous to other players. Before each match the referee or touch-judges will inspect the studs to ensure that they are safe.

The standard numbering system for all International Board games is as follows.

*THE STANDARD NUMBERING SYSTEM FOR ALL INTERNATIONAL BOARD RUGBY LEAGUE GAMES*

**1** – Full-back
**2** – Right wing three-quarter
**3** – Centre three-quarter
**4** – Centre three-quarter
**5** – Left wing three-quarter
**6** – Stand-off half
**7** – Scrum-half
**8** – Open-side prop
**9** – Hooker

**10** – Blind-side prop
**11** – Second-row forward
**12** – Second-row forward
**13** – Loose forward
**14** – Back-division substitute
**15** – Back-division substitute
**16** – Forward substitute
**17** – Forward substitute

Different systems can be employed if allowed by the national governing body and, in Britain, the European Super League allows each player to have his or her own individual squad number.

# TERMINOLOGY

**Acting half-back**  A player who stands behind the ball-carrier when he is tackled and then plays the ball.

**Advantage**  Referees can allow play to continue if it is to the advantage of the team who has not committed the offence or infringement.

**Back**  A member of a team who plays as a half-back, three-quarter or full-back.

**Ball back**  If the ball goes into touch without bouncing, it is returned to the point where it was kicked and play re-starts with a scrummage to the opposing team.

**Blind side**  If the play is taking place near one side of the field, the shorter side to the touch-line is known as the blind side.

**Blood bin**  If a player is injured and bleeding the referee has the power to send him off the field of play to receive treatment. No player is allowed to continue playing while bleeding heavily. A player sent to the blood bin can return to the field as soon as the bleeding has stopped or dressing applied. He may be replaced while being treated but his replacement must leave once he returns.

**Bomb**  The Australian term used for an up-and-under kick.

**Broken play**  When play is taking place outside a set-piece situation, e.g. a scrummage.

**Caution**  Warning a player receives if the referee decides that his personal foul or persistent infringing has to be officially noted in his notebook for recording to the League disciplinary authority.

**Charge down**  This happens when a player kicks the ball and a defender knocks it down.

**Converting a try**  The act of kicking a goal after a try has been scored.

**Cover-tackle**  Tackling an attacking player who has broken through the defensive line.

**Crossing/Shepherding**  The act of deliberate obstruction by attacking players. The passer continues running into the path of would-be tacklers to protect his team-mate. Known as 'shepherding' in Australia. This is an infringement.

**Dead ball**  Any ball that goes out of play.

**Differential penalty**  After a technical infringement at a scrummage the referee awards a penalty but it does not entitle the non-offending team to kick for goal and score. They have the option to kick for touch or tap to re-start.

**Drop goal/Field goal**  The scoring of a goal from open play by means of a drop kick. Known as a field goal in Australia.

**Drop kick**  A kick made by dropping the ball from the hands and making contact with the foot as soon as the ball hits the ground.

**Drop out**  A means of bringing the ball back into play. It is a drop kick taken from either between the posts or from the centre of the 20-metre line.

**Dummy**  An attacking player holds the ball after pretending to pass it with the object of deceiving the defenders.

**Dummy half**  see Acting half-back.

**Feeding the scrum**  When the scrum-half places the ball into the tunnel between the two sets of forwards at a scrummage. Feeding is also a term used to describe an infringement at the scrummage when scrum-halves deliberately slant the ball in to their own forwards' feet.

**Flopper**  A player falling on an attacking player who has already been stopped.

**Forward**  A player who operates in the scrummage.

**Forward pass**  An infringement when a player throws the ball forward towards his opponents' goal-line.

**Free kick**  The kick awarded to a team which kicks into touch from a penalty. Taken 10m (11yd) opposite where the ball crosses the touch-line, it can be kicked in any direction but you cannot score.

**Full-time** The end of a game after 80 minutes.

**Hand over** When a team has retained the ball for six tackles and is then forced to give the ball to their opponents.

**Heel** When a player pushes the ball behind himself with his heel or boot sole.

**Hook** When a hooker pulls the ball back in the scrummage.

**Kick-off** When the match is started with a kick from the centre spot.

**Knock-on** An infringement when a player knocks the ball towards his opponents' goal-line with his arm or hand.

**Loose arm** An offence when the hooker packs down in the scrum with one arm not correctly bound round the prop forward.

**Loose ball** When the ball is not held by a player or being scrum-maged.

**Loose head** The prop forward nearest the referee at a scrummage.

**Mark** The point from which a penalty is taken, or where a scrum is formed.

**Obstruction** When a player deliberately impedes an opponent not in possession of the ball.

**Offside** A law applied when a player is temporarily out of the play and may be penalized if he joins in the game.

**On-field report** If a referee suspects that there has been an element of foul play but is not in a position to make a decision on who is at fault, he can mark the point in the game by signalling with arms crossed above his head. As every professional game is video-recorded the governing body can then analyze the incident to decide whether any player involved in the incident has to be referred to the Disciplinary Commitee.

**On the full**  Used when the ball crosses any line without bouncing.

**Onside**  Used when a player is not offside.

**Open side**  The side of the scrum or play-the-ball on the far side from the touch-line. Opposite to Blind side.

**Pack**  A common term used to describe one team's forwards.

**Pass**  Throwing the ball from one player to another.

**Penalize**  When the referee awards a penalty kick against an offending player.

**Penalty kick**  A type of free kick awarded to the non-offending team after an offence has been committed.

**Place kick**  Describes a kick where the ball is placed on the ground before being kicked.

**Play-the-ball**  The way to bring the ball back into play after a tackle is completed.

**Punt**  Kicking the ball from the hands without it hitting the ground.

**Put-in**  see Feeding the scrum.

**Ruck**  A group of players contesting possession.

**Scrum, Scrummage or Scrimmage**  The two sets of forwards directly facing each other to contest possession.

**Second movement**  When a grounded player reaches over the goal-line after he has been tackled to touch the ball down.

**Sin bin**  Where a player is sent after being temporarily dismissed.

**Spot tackling**  The system of man-to-man marking when defenders take one of their opponents as a special responsibility.

**Stealing**  The act of taking the ball from a player before the tackle is called 'as complete'.

**Strike**  The action of a hooker attempting to pull the ball back with his feet in the scrum.

**Tap kick**  When a team opts for tapping the ball on a kicker's boot to re-start the game. The ball can travel in any direction, and any player, including the kicker, may gather the ball.

**Touch-down**  When a defending player grounds the ball in his own in-goal area.

**Touch in-goal**  When a player steps outside the pitch limits while in the in-goal area.

**Try**  The act of grounding the ball in the in-goal area for a score.

**Upright tackle**  Describes a tackle when both players remain on their feet.

**Zero tackle**  An attacking team is allowed to carry the ball for six tackles before they hand it over to the opposition. If a team received the ball from a kick downfield by the previous ball-carriers and the player who catches the ball is subsequently tackled, it does not register in the tackle count.

# The game – a guide

**Rugby League is a game designed for two teams of players each with thirteen players on the pitch at any one time. Each team must be dressed in separate, differently coloured outfits.**

Four players are named as substitutes before the start of the game and teams can make up to six interchanges with these players through the game. National governing bodies have the power to allow substitution laws to be varied.

The game is governed by a referee assisted by two touch-judges and, in many top-class matches, two in-goal judges. In both codes of Rugby, League and Union, players are noted for their acceptance of refereeing decisions; dissent is not acceptable behaviour.

The object of any game of Rugby League is to score more points than the opposing side. Players carry the oval-shaped ball towards their opponents' end of the pitch by passing the ball with their hands to team-mates or kicking it. There are two ways to score: a try or a goal. A try is scored when a player crosses the opposing team's goal-line and grounds the ball.

A team receives four points for scoring a try no matter where the ball is grounded in the in-goal area. After a try the scoring team is then allowed to go for two extra points by kicking the ball off the ground from a point level with the place it was grounded. The extra points are awarded if the ball goes between the posts and over the crossbar, in what is known as a conversion.

There are two other varieties of goal. At any time during open play a player may drop the ball on the ground and, once it has bounced, kick it through the upper half of the posts. This is known as a drop, or field, goal and it is worth one point. There is also the penalty goal. This is awarded if a player is judged to have committed a personal foul against an opponent or a technical infringement of the laws. The only time that does not apply is when the referee awards a differential penalty which is given for an infringement of a scrummage law. In Rugby League a penalty goal is worth two points and is scored by kicking the ball off the ground and over the crossbar.

Play in senior Rugby League matches lasts for 80 minutes, divided into two equal halves, with a five-minute interval between the two. A team captain, a player nominated by the club at professional level or elected by the other players in amateur teams, will meet his opposite number just before the start of a match. Watched by the referee, they will toss a coin to decide who kicks off. The home captain tosses and the away captain 'calls'. The winner chooses which end to defend first while the loser kicks off.

*Paying the penalty. This is what happens when a penalty kick is taken*

*It's a try! A player dives over the line to put the ball down for four points*

The referee wears a uniform designated by the ruling League and it must be in complete contrast to those uniforms worn by the opposing teams. He starts the game by blowing a whistle when he is satisfied that both teams are ready to start the game.

The referee has a very responsible job. He is in charge of the game and must ensure that the laws are obeyed and that maximum consideration is given to the safety of the players. He starts and

*Ready for the kick-off. Note the position of each player just before the start of a game. The numbers in circles indicate the attacking side while those in squares are defenders*

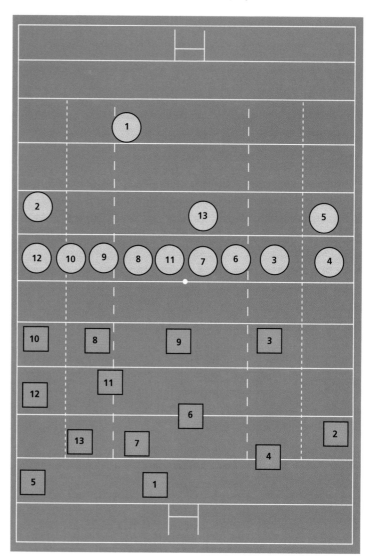

stops the game with a whistle. In the professional game he receives a signal from two time-keepers at the side of the pitch when it is half-time and when the game is completed. In the amateur game the referee generally controls time-keeping with at least one reliable watch. He also carries a notebook to record the score and official cautions of players for breaches of discipline.

Referees are assisted in most matches by two touch-judges and, in top-class matches, by two in-goal judges. They each have a flag, usually one red and one orange, and their job is to mark the place on the edge of the pitch where the ball passes out of play, mark the 10-metre point at penalty situations and help the referee by observing players' behaviour when they are out of the referee's vision. After a try or following the award of a penalty, the touch-judges have to stand behind the goal-posts; if the ball goes correctly between the posts, they hold their flags up, and if the kick fails they wave them close to the ground.

In-goal judges assist the referee by paying attention to play when it moves in the in-goal area. They are useful in providing an alternative view when the referee is unsighted by a number of players or unsure if a try has been scored. For televised matches an extra referee sits behind a television screen away from the pitch and is available to aid any referee who calls for a slow-motion replay of the incident to help him make a decision.

All thirteen players must be in their correct half of the pitch before a game can start. The player who takes the kick-off has to make sure that the ball goes 10m (34ft) into his opponents' half and stays on the pitch. If he fails on either count, his opponents receive a penalty kick on the centre spot from which they can score – if they have a player who can kick that far!

Usually a player will direct his starting kick across to one of the wings. The opposing team's set of six forwards try to position themselves under where the ball will land while the kicker's forwards charge at them trying either to take the ball themselves or prevent the receiving players from starting an attack.

There are two distinct phases of play in Rugby League. A team either has possession of the ball or it is defending. Let us now run through an imaginary game so that the significance of the two phases can be fully understood. After the kick-off from the centre spot the defending players catch the ball. The player in possession can run forward, attempt to break through the defence and then, at any stage while he is making progress, pass the ball to one of his team-mates. But he is restricted to passing the ball backwards and in *no* other direction. If the referee thinks he has passed forward deliberately he can award a penalty.

The defending players can try to stop the ball-carrier by tackling him to the ground. A tackle can be made in any way a defender chooses, with the following restrictions:

a. Only the ball-carrier can be tackled.

b. A tackle must be made below the head.

c. A ball-carrier cannot be tripped.

d. No blow must be made with the fist or any other foul tactic used.

Once a ball-carrier is taken to the ground or his progress is stopped completely he has to play-the-ball to re-start play. Should there be any doubt the referee will call 'Held' to indicate that the tackle is complete. If the ball-carrier's team retain possession for four more play-the-balls they are then faced with a decision.

If they hold on for one more tackle, and a player *is* tackled, then they must hand the ball over to their opponents. Regaining possession is obviously difficult. The alternative to risking another tackle is a long kick upfield, which will certainly keep the opposing team deep in their own half, and could possibly lead to them making an error.

*Play-the-ball. One of Rugby League's vital skills*

Players will evade the tacklers for as long as possible to avoid being stopped. They can move the ball around with passes and, once a gap in the defence is created, send one of their team through to attempt a score. The only time that the game is ever halted is when a player in possession infringes a law or after foul play.

For technical offences the referee awards a scrummage to re-start the game. This is when six forwards bind together in a triangular shape and the front row of three inter-lock their heads with their opposing numbers. The ball is fed into the gap between them with possession going to the side whose hooker can pull the ball into their side.

Like soccer, the game of Rugby League has its offside law. Although it appears quite complicated at first, it is basically quite simple. When the game requires a play-the-ball, i.e. after a completed tackle, the defending side must be 5m (16ft) away or they are offside. A player is also offside if he seeks to gain an advantage by interfering in front of his team when they are holding the ball.

At the start of the second half the teams switch direction and play continues until the time-keepers or referee decide that the 80 minutes have been completed. If players are injured and the referee

*Caught out! Player B is offside*

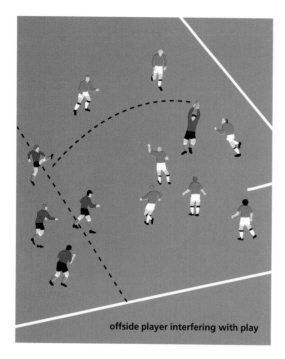

offside player interfering with play

tackling from offside position

**Above:** *The player catching his team-mate's kick is offside*
**Above right:** *Tackling the player catching the ball in advance of the kicker is offside until the player in possession has run 10m (34ft)*

has to stop the game, the time it takes either to remove the player from the pitch or complete his treatment is added on at the end of each half. If a penalty is awarded and then the hooter or whistle is sounded, the non-offending side can take the kick.

In addition to breaching the laws a player can be penalized by the referee for bad behaviour. There is a code of ten offences that players must not commit and they are:

**1** Tripping or striking another player.
**2** Attacking an opponent's head when making a tackle.
**3** Dropping the knees on a player who is on the ground.
**4** Using a dangerous throw, e.g. of a martial arts kind, in a tackle.
**5** Deliberately breaking the Laws of the Game.
**6** Using offensive language.
**7** Disputing the decision of the referee or touch-judges.
**8** Re-entering the field of play after a temporary absence without permission of the referee or touch-judge.
**9** Behaving against the spirit of the game.
**10** Deliberately obstructing an opponent who is not in possession.

If a player is penalized for any breach of behaviour the referee can award a penalty against his team which would cost them points if the opposition kick the goal. Or he may send the offending player to the sin bin for ten minutes and that would leave the team short of men. Alternatively he could send the player from the pitch completely and the player would then have to appear before the League Disciplinary Committee, which would probably suspend him. If the referee was uncertain which player was at fault, he can cross his arms above his heads, thus signalling an on-field report.

Kicking plays an important part in modern Rugby League. Although it is essentially a handling game and by far the largest part of it is spent in passing the ball, the science of kicking the oval ball is nevertheless an important part of a team's armoury.

The ball cannot be kicked directly into touch to make ground, except with a penalty kick. In League the advantage will go to the kicking side only if the ball bounces on the playing side of the touch-line before going into touch.

*Some of the signals given by a referee: player penalized for dissent (left); and scrum-half illegally feeding his own forwards at a scrummage (centre). Touch-judge indicating the place where the ball passed over the touch-line (right)*

A penalty kick can be taken in two ways. Either a player can place the ball on the ground to attempt a shot at goal or he can kick the ball directly into touch. If the second option is taken, the player can kick the ball either off the ground or out of his hands. If the ball goes into touch, the game is re-started with a tap kick opposite where the ball went out of play.

You will always know what is happening when the referee makes a decision because he makes a signal to the spectators to indicate the offence which has been penalized. There are forty-four such signals and most of them make it quite plain which offence has happened. The touch-judges too have a limited number of signals which they make to indicate circumstances to the referee.

*More referee signals: forward pass (left); obstruction (centre); and hooker's foot up too early at scrummage (right)*

*George Mann of Leeds beats his way through Wigan's defence during a home match at Headingley*

# Rules clinic

Like all other team sports Rugby League is governed by an international set of rules. These are designed to ensure that each match is played under the same conditions and that players are afforded maximum possible safety.

**What happens to a team after they have had six successive tackles against them?**
They have to hand the ball over to the opposing team and the game is re-started with a play-the-ball. Professional teams hate giving the ball away without having a chance of regaining it so they usually opt to kick the ball after the fifth tackle. This has the effect of forcing the opposition to start their tackle sequence as far away from the kicker's line as possible; it also gives the kicking side the chance to regain possession if their opponents infringe or make a mistake under pressure from players who have followed up the kick downfield. If during the tackle sequence an opponent touches the ball in any way, the referee can order the count to start again.

**In the previous chapter it was mentioned that a triangle of forwards face each other in a scrummage. How do you decide**

*The placing for the forwards at the scrummage for each direction of play*

*Side view of the forwards at a scrummage*

**which set of forwards have the advantage of the head on the outside?**

In 1988, the International Board, the game's law-making body, decreed that in every scrummage – for whatever reason – the non-offending side will have the advantage of the prop forward nearest to the scrum-half.

**Can a referee allow any advantage?**

Most certainly. Although it is not written into the laws of the game the referee has total discretion. If it is obvious that the non-offending team can gain an advantage by play continuing, the referee can allow the game to carry on. And that does not mean that the offending player gets away with it. When the play sequence ends a referee can penalize him at that point.

**If a ball drops on the touch-line is it in play or out?**

In Rugby League the touch-line is counted as out of the field of play. The same applies to the touch in-goal and the dead-ball lines. The goal-line counts as the in-goal area, and if a player grounds the ball on that line it counts as a try.

**Are there any restrictions on the movements of players and can they all score?**

The answers are no and yes. All twenty-six players on the pitch can move anywhere they wish and they can all score tries and goals.

**How do the players know when to play the ball?**

When an attacking player is not making progress in a tackle he has to play the ball but the referee will shout 'Held' indicating that the tackle is complete if there is any doubt. The defenders then have to retreat 10m (32ft) except for one man who will face the player in possession. Until the start of the 1988–89 season the defending player could be supported by a team-mate but, after a year-long experiment, it was disallowed. The attacker then places the ball down on the ground and drags it back with his foot to a team-mate behind him known as the 'acting half-back'. The defender may attempt to hook the ball back as soon as the ball touches the ground.

**Is it possible to be ruled offside at a play-the-ball situation?**

This is one of the biggest sources of dispute at any level of Rugby League. At the play-the-ball the referee will mark 10m (32ft) from the tackled players and the defenders must return to that mark. If they are caught encroaching, the referee will penalize the player concerned and award a penalty against him. If the ball is kicked downfield and players on the kicking side reach the player who catches it before his own team-mates can support him, they can be offside. They have to allow him to kick the ball or to run 10m (32ft) unhindered. Equally, if the player catching the ball fails to hold it and one of his team-mates grabs it without first getting behind the player who dropped it, he too would be offside.

In its simplest form you must be between your team-mate and your goal-line to receive the ball and remain onside. Offside is punishable by a penalty but if you are *accidentally* caught in an offside position, the referee can order a scrummage.

**If a player about to score a try is badly obstructed or personally fouled, what happens?**
Quite simply the referee awards the try if he is satisfied that the player concerned was certain to score. This is called a penalty try and no matter where the offence takes place it is always awarded under the posts, making life much easier for the goal-kicker. If the player is personally fouled during or just after the act of scoring the referee can award a penalty which is taken immediately after the conversion from in front of the posts.

**What happens if a player is injured during the game?**
Usually, injured players are treated on the field of play while the game continues. But if it is clear that by continuing the game the safety and well-being of that player would be endangered the referee can call a halt and stop the game-clock, making the necessary signal to the time-keepers. If after treatment a player in possession cannot immediately play the ball the laws have now been adjusted so that he can hand the ball over to a team-mate to re-start the game.

**Sometimes local dignitaries kick a match off. Does that count as the start of the game?**
No, it does not! The ball must be returned to the centre spot for the game to start with a proper kick-off.

**If you have just scored a try does it matter where you place the ball for a conversion attempt?**
Kickers have some discretion so that they can achieve a more favourable angle. They can place the ball at any point on an

*A goal-kick after a try has been scored*

imaginary line running parallel with the touch-line from the place where the try was scored. A touch-judge will mark the position where the line has to start and when the kicker is ready to take his shot the official moves behind the posts.

For a goal to count the ball must completely cross the crossbar and be kicked on the full without being touched in flight by an opponent. Incidentally, unlike Rugby Union, in Rugby League it is illegal to distract the goal-kicker by charging at him during a conversion attempt. In the professional game touch-judges indicate if a goal-kick is successful but the referee is the sole judge. And his decision is final.

**In Rugby League the game is sometimes re-started with a drop kick from under the posts. When does this happen?**

In the Laws there are seven instances. Basically they all relate to happenings in the in-goal area. For example, if one player kicks a loose ball over the dead-ball line or touches down a loose ball in his own in-goal area this is the way to re-start play. It is also used if a defender infringes or is tackled in the in-goal area. If an attacker infringes in the in-goal area or is the last to touch the ball before it goes over the dead-ball or touch-in-goal line, then the defending side can kick the ball off with a place kick at the 20-metre line. If, after an unsuccessful goal-kick the ball goes dead, the defending side can re-start play with a drop kick from the centre of the 20-metre line.

**Tackling is an essential part of the game. Is there any way you cannot ground an opponent?**

Yes, despite its appearance the art of tackling is very disciplined. It has to be for the safety of all the players concerned. You are not allowed to use your knees or employ any special throws or holds, e.g. of a martial arts kind, which are liable to cause injury. You can use your leg to bring an opponent over providing your arms make contact with him first. You are not permitted to go above the shoulder line in a tackle. Dismissal from the field can follow a deliberately high tackle.

**How does a referee decide you have knocked the ball on?**

The criteria for his decision are quite simple and straightforward.

*Saved! A player fails to take posses-sion and re-gathers the ball at the second attempt*

He will penalize you if he thinks that you have deliberately knocked the ball forward or passed forward. A knock-on is where you hit the ball with your hand or arm and it goes to ground.

     If you fail to hold the ball and re-gather it after it goes to ground then the referee will award a scrummage with head and feed to your opponents. If, after knocking the ball on, it doesn't touch the floor or a goal-post or crossbar you will be allowed to carry on in possession. By the way, if you charge down an opponent's kick that will not be judged as a knock-on.

**An attacking player passes the ball close to his opponents' line and it rebounds from his team-mate's head on to the floor. Can the first player re-gather and score?**
Yes, the try stands. As long as his team-mate did not touch it with his hands or arms it does not matter from which part of the body the ball rebounds.

**If a full-back catches the ball in the in-goal area can his opponents try to tackle or dispossess him?**
Until recently they could. But, in view of the danger to any player up in the air trying to catch a high kick under pressure from several attacking players, it was decided that if the full-back held the ball cleanly he should remain unmolested and his skill should be

rewarded by being allowed to re-start the game with a tap kick on the 20-metre line.

**As a player rises to play-the-ball he puts his foot on the touch-line. Can he continue?**

Yes, he is allowed to play-the-ball.

**If a referee sends a player to the sin bin how do you know when he will return to the game?**

In Britain the referee will dismiss the player and then hold up a coloured card. The yellow card indicates a ten-minute absence. Alternately he can signal with ten fingers.

**What happens if a player kicks the ball and it doesn't bounce before going into touch?**

If the ball goes out without first bouncing on the pitch then it is brought back to where the kick was made and a scrum formed. If it bounces off a player following a kick then the scrum takes place where it hit him.

Right: *Finding touch. Note the ball bouncing before leaving the pitch*
Right below: *Ball back. The kicker puts the ball directly out of play*

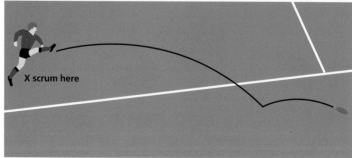

**If a player is tackled short of the line but slides into the in-goal area, does it count as a try?**

Yes, it does. If his momentum following the tackle carries him over the line and he is neither in touch nor touch in-goal then the score is good. If he comes to a halt in a tackle just before the line and then reaches over he will be penalized for making a second movement. Should the ball not be grounded then he could try to continue because the tackle was not complete.

**How much power does a referee have in Rugby League?**

Total control. He is appointed to be the guardian of the Laws and his control starts even before a player sets foot on the pitch. He is in charge of them from the moment they come into the playing area until the second they leave. Anybody else who wants to come on to the pitch must have his permission.

In professional Rugby he will have the help of two touch-judges but that is not always so in amateur games. He is the only official allowed to award tries or goals, although he may take advice from a touch-judge if he is unsighted by the action of play. He has the power to suspend play for whatever reason, for example because of adverse weather conditions, undue interference from spectators, misbehaviour by the players or anything else that inter-feres with the game.

He has the authority to send players off the pitch for misbe-haviour or persistent transgression of the laws. And he can dismiss them permanently or for temporary spells of ten minutes in the sin bin. He controls the game with the aid of a whistle and he will sound it for six reasons.

1 A try or goal has been scored.
2 The ball has gone out of play.
3 He sees a breach of the laws except when advantage applies.
4 If the ball or the player comes into contact irregularly with the referee, touch-judge or anybody not officially connected with the game or an object that should not be on the pitch.
5 When anything not provided for in the Laws happens and a team gets an unfair advantage.
6 When a stoppage is necessary to enforce the Laws or for any other reason.

Once a referee has made a decision he cannot change it and that is why it is useless trying to pressurize him with dissent. The only exception to that situation is when a touch-judge reports an incident of foul play that the referee did not see before making his decision. Being a Rugby League referee is not an easy job. For example, he has to keep a count of all the completed tackles while play is in motion, signal his decisions and carry a huge responsibility. To reach the level of the professional game he has to pass a series of examinations and reach either Grade 1 or 2. And, at each professional game, there will be an assessor who watches his performance and monitors the quality of his application of the Laws.

*A penalty kick to the touch-line*

**Is there any occasion when you can kick the ball directly into touch?**

Yes. When you are awarded a penalty. From that point, assuming it is not a differential penalty, there is a choice: a kick at goal for two points or the option of gaining ground. If you decide on the latter then you can put the ball into touch on the full and then re-start the game with a tap kick from the point level with where the ball went into touch.

**If a team receives a ball after a 'hand-over' does the play-the-ball that re-starts the game count as one of their sequence?**

No, it does not. The referee will start counting their conceded tackles from the moment the game is re-started. The referee will indicate when the sequence is coming to an end because at the fifth tackle he will put his hand straight up into the air and shout 'Last'. Then a team will have to decide whether to kick the ball or risk another tackle and hand the ball over. If during a sequence the defending team touches the ball but fails to retain it, the referee can nullify the count and start again at once. A riccochet or rebound off a player does not count as a 'touch' and players cannot gain an advantage by kicking the ball against an opponent.

**What is a differential penalty?**

This penalty can only be awarded for a scrum offence and the only difference between it and a normal penalty is that you do not have the option of kicking at goal. To re-start the game the non-offending team has to kick the ball into touch or take a tap kick.

But that does not mean that every offence at a scrummage will be punished with a differential penalty. The referee can still award a normal penalty against any player for foul play and offside.

**Can you play the ball to yourself and play on?**
No, you must play the ball.

**Where does the non-feeding scrum-half stand at a scrummage?**
The non-feeding scrum-half should retire behind the pack like all the other players not involved in the scrummage. All the players outside the scrum must retire by 5m (16ft) until the ball has emerged.

**What happens if a player is caught in an offside position through no fault of his own?**
If the player concerned comes into contact with a ball-carrier or the ball the referee can allow play to continue if no attempt is made to play or interfere with the game. But if the player in the offside positions gains an advantage for his side a scrum must be formed with head and ball going to the non-offending team. The referee will not penalize the player for being accidentally offside. It is possible for a player to take possession of the ball and not realize that he is in an offside position; if the referee believes the player did not know he was offside, he can rule it as accidental.

**Can you be offside in your own in-goal area?**
You cannot be offside in your own in-goal area but you can be penalized in your opponent's.

**If a trainer runs on to the field of play to treat an injured player and collides with an attacking player, what happens?**
The game must be re-started with a play-the-ball which does not count in the attacking team's sequence.

**An attacking player kicks the ball ahead and a defender charges it down. The player who kicked re-gathers the ball and continues the attack. What is the referee's ruling?**
The teams play on and the tackle count is set back, if necessary, to one in favour of the attacking team. If the defender had succeeded

*Charging a kick down*

in holding the ball or gained possession of it, the referee would also have allowed the teams to play on. A charge-down of a kick does not count as a knock-on.

**A player catches a penalty kick on the full but his foot is on the touch-line. What happens next?**
The second phase of the penalty applies because the player who caught the ball was in touch. The line markings are out of play. If the player had caught the ball on the dead-ball line after it had been kicked during open play the defending team would have been given the ball to re-start the game with a place kick from the centre of the 20-metre line. The situation is judged to be the same as if the attacking team had kicked the ball dead behind their opponents' line.

**If the hooter goes after the award of a penalty, can the kick still be taken?**
If it is a place kick the team awarded the penalty have the option to kick at goal and the score would count. Alternatively they could choose the tap penalty and attempt to score a try, which would

count. The play in that case would be ended if the defenders could complete a tackle before the attacking side scored.

**If a player who has knocked the ball forward is prevented from picking it up by an opponent, will play continue?**
No, because the team who lost possession will receive a penalty. You cannot obstruct an opponent not in possession, even one who is offside or trying to regain a ball that has been knocked off.

**What happens when you kick at goal and the wind blows the ball back across the crossbar?**
There's no need to worry because the goal still stands. As long as the whole of the ball crosses the bar the score has been correctly made.

**Would the referee allow a try to be scored if during a scrum near the line the attacking side push over the goal-line and drop on the ball?**
No, you cannot score in a scrummage. But if the ball comes out at the rear of the attacking side's pack and one of their players charges through the rest of his forwards to touch down then the try would be allowed.

# Technique

Rugby League is becoming increasingly popular because it demands great quantities of skill, fitness, courage and, most of all, teamwork.

Whatever level of the game you come into contact with it is essential that you have some command of the techniques needed to play a useful part in a team effort. There will always be some players in a side who are blessed with more skills and talent than the rest but they are not likely to function properly if the other players in the team cannot fulfill the simple necessities of the game.

Broken down into basic requirements Rugby League players should be able to catch and run with the ball, pass it to a colleague and tackle. If you can perform all those functions adequately then the only other problem you have is choosing which position you are best suited to. Of course, when it comes to actually playing the game there is much more to consider, but without those three basic skills your progress and enjoyment of the game will be necessarily limited.

Each of those elements can be performed at a basic level in

your early matches. Once you have learned them, then you are in a position to develop them in such a way that you can add considerable variety and effectiveness to both the team's and your personal performance. This is what we mean by technique. What you have to remember about Rugby League is that you have two distinct phases: attack, when you are in possession, and defence, when the opposition have the ball. Each phase requires different skills from the players and that is why it is so important to listen to your team coach or teacher. They have the advantage of being able to look on at a game and see how your performance is fitting in.

The ball is in play for a considerable amount of time in Rugby League and it is important for you to pay great attention to your personal fitness. As well as ensuring that you will be able to last through the full 80 minutes, contributing all the time, being fit will also reduce your chances of serious injury. League is a hard, physical game – there is no disguising that fact – but you can reduce the risks to yourself if you are in good shape. Clearly, the higher up the ladder you go the more is asked of you in training. Professional players are given fitness programmes for the winter break while top amateur players in the elite National League train almost as hard as the professionals. At other levels, the requirements are more basic but just as important.

Tactics have always been important in Rugby League, and in the modern game with its limited number of tackles they have become even more crucial. The side who controls the ball have a better than even chance of winning the game, so it follows that the team with the more skilful players are more likely to control possession for longer.

# PASSING & HANDLING

The first skill you will need is to be able to pass the ball effectively in either direction. You are a passenger if you cannot give the ball to somebody else when you are tackled, or when a team-mate is better placed or in order to move the ball to a superior tactical position.

Once you have the ball in your hands you are the centre of attraction. Defenders will be looking to stop you or to make you

**HOLDING A RUGBY BALL**
**Right:** *How to hold the ball from above. See the thumb placings*
**Far right:** *Notice the spread of the fingers under the ball*

drop it while your team-mates expect to receive a good, accurate pass. It is essential to have a well-rehearsed, consistent grip on the ball. Imagine you are making a cradle shape with your hands and lower arms. Grip the ball with your fingers spread out on the under part while using your thumbs to hold on to the upper portion. Your arms should be relaxed and bent slightly from the elbow so that you can swing the ball in either direction. Your thumbs hold the ball securely in position and you should be able to move it up and down as well as across your body.

Now that you feel comfortable holding the ball, try running up and down the pitch with it so that you become accustomed to the action. Passing has two phases. First you have to deliver the ball to a team-mate. Assuming that you are holding it properly you have to take aim and this means that you have to keep an eye on the target. Years of experience show that the ideal place for a pass to be received is called the 'bread basket', located between the lower chest and waist.

Keeping your eye on that target, twist from the waist and swing your arms well back. Now bring your arms back across your body and let the ball go towards the target area making sure that on release it travels in front of the man or woman you are passing to. You will be able to direct the ball with your wrists and fingers, but bear in mind that the speed of your pass will be dictated by how far in front of the player you need to direct the ball. Clearly the faster the receiver is going the more you must aim in front of him or her.

Once you have let the ball go, follow through with your arms so that they are fully extended towards the receiver with the fingers pointing at the target. Keeping this in mind helps both your action and direction.

That is one half of the art of passing. As well as giving passes you have to be able to receive them. It is no use being a member of any team if you cannot hold the ball regularly when it is passed to you. Once you think that a player is likely to pass the ball to you it is time to start your preparations. It may take only a fraction of a second but the same principles are always observed. First, you must not take your eye off your team-mate no matter what is going on around you. Move your arms and hands out with fingers extended to face the passer. It always helps if you use both hands but in some circumstances this is not possible. If you are forced to use one hand then apply the same method. Once the ball reaches you it should be

**PASSING THE BALL**
Left: *Pull the arms back when ready to pass and note the position of the feet when passing left*
Right: *Keep your eyes on the intended receiver*

brought into your body. This will help you bring it under control and prepare you to pass it on if required. If you grip the ball in the same way as you did when you were passing it, a tackler will find it less easy to dislodge.

There are two things to keep in mind. You must be ready to catch a badly directed pass and to receive the ball unexpectedly. Quite often the ball is released at an unlikely moment; if it surprises you, no doubt it will be doing the same to the opposition. By catching it cleanly, though, you retain possession and the initiative for your team.

When you come to deliver your passes during play, you will inevitably be running. When you are passing to the left you should aim to pass when the right leg is leading and vice versa when you move the ball to the right. This will give you more twist in your body and greater accuracy to your pass.

Experience and practice will teach you when a pass is necessary, and there is one golden rule which your team-mates will always appreciate your remembering. That is, 'Never pass to somebody in a worse position than yourself.' If your colleague is well marked it is better to absorb the tackle and seek a better position for your team after a play-the-ball. This is one reason why, once the ball is in your hands, you must be aware of the game around you. It is no use, for example, hanging on to the ball while the defence becomes organized. Think too of the possibilities offered by a long pass. You can sometimes take the opposition completely by surprise by lofting the ball over the head of your nearest team-mate to one beyond. At the same time, though, a pass of that kind is easier to intercept, so you should use it only when you are certain of reaching your man.

Never forget that in Rugby you can only pass backwards. At first it can seem difficult but, after practice, it becomes second nature. In League the act of passing is not restricted to just running movements. You may be called upon to take up a position as acting half-back, and it is advisable to be proficient at passing from the ground. When you do this, make sure you know exactly where your receiver is and how much weight you will need to put into the pass. Bend well over the ball and, taking a firm grip, prepare to make the pass. Turn your body towards your receiver and pass from the ground, ensuring that you do not straighten your back but stay on

*The dotted line shows a legal pass and one which is forward*

**PASSING FROM THE GROUND**
*Keep your eyes firmly fixed on the ball ...*

*... Straddle the ball with your hands ...*

your feet. Again the ball is directed with your fingers and wrists with a well-defined follow-through.

Not that you can always take the ball off the floor in such controlled circumstances. If you see a loose ball, the chances are that if you run straight at it your boot will make contact first. Run alongside and scoop it up, running your hand underneath so that you can exert some grip at the same time. The key to the whole operation is concentration; keep your eye firmly fixed on the ball.

*... Grip the ball firmly and look at the player you want to find*

A bouncing ball represents a real problem. There is a saying in both codes of Rugby: 'Never let the ball bounce.' Because of its shape you can never tell which direction it will take. When you have to retrieve a ball that has bounced keep your eye on it all the time – it's the only chance you have.

Now that long, high kicks have become common in the League game it is important that every player is able to deal with them. The art requires concentration, judgment and confidence. As soon as you see a high ball heading your way position yourself underneath and form your arms into a cradle with your fingertips

**CATCHING A HIGH BALL**
Far left: *Cradle your arms and watch the ball*
Left: *Pull the ball into your chest, keeping your elbows together*

facing the ball. When the ball makes contact with you, absorb the shock with your body and then wrap your arms around it. In other words, cuddle it. Keep your elbows in front of your body, although not too far apart or it will drop through the gap. Many players prefer to jump to meet the ball. This is a decisive approach which needs care, co-ordination and plenty of practice.

**PLAYING-THE-BALL**
*Playing-the-ball properly is essential in Rugby League. Hold the ball firmly as you place it on the ground, roll it firmly along the ground to the player behind and perform the movement as quickly as possible*

# PLAY-THE-BALL

The act of play-the-ball is a two-man scrummage. It is one of the distinctive plays that is particular to Rugby League and it has its own set of skills that players have to master.

 The moment you are tackled in possession of the ball you have two choices. You can pass if you are still able to or you must absorb the tackle and play-the-ball. There are likely to be around 300 play-the-balls in a match, so it is a skill you cannot take lightly.

 Speed is essential. A ball played slowly gives the opposition a chance to re-group and prepare for your team's next drive forward. Once the tackled player hits the ground or the referee calls 'Held', it

*The play-the-ball sequence from the side*

is up to the ball-carrier to get to his feet as quickly as possible. He should lift the ball clear of the ground, taking care not to knock-on, and face his opponent's goal-line. The next move is important. Bend well over the ball and place it lengthways on the floor next to your leading foot. Then release it. At the same time put your other foot on top of the ball and roll it back to the player who has taken up position behind you as acting half-back. The danger point for the ball-carrier is when the ball is being placed on the ground and he may lose control of it unless he is vigilant.

# TACKLING

Having looked at how you play with the ball in your hands, now we must consider what happens when it is your turn to defend. Your team is now lined up across the pitch facing the opposition. It is your job to stop them breaking through and to ensure that they do not make progress while in possession. As a bonus you will be trying to dislodge the ball so that you can start an attack.

Tackling is not just a question of leaping on another player to inflict the maximum possible damage or pain. You have to be firm and resolute but not cruel. It also requires skill and courage to tackle properly without hurting yourself, and you should think about and practise your tackling regularly.

The objects of a tackle in Rugby League are three-fold. First, to stop the man making progress. Second, to prevent him from passing to a colleague and, third, to force him to lose possession. To achieve any of these three you must deliver your tackle with deter-mination. The best way to go in is hard and low. When a player in possession is running towards you, put yourself in a position to intercept. Your target area is the thigh, and remember at all times to keep your head to one side of the ball-carrier. Drive your

*Notice tackler's shoulder aimed at the thigh*

shoulder into the attacker and enircle his thighs with your arms. Once you have established a grip slide down the carrier's legs taking him to the ground. The tackler should end up on top of the carrier. If the tackle is done correctly the carrier will not have had time to release a pass and be forced to play-the-ball.

Clearly not every tackle will take place under perfect circumstances. In general players have to make the contact from one of three directions: from the front, from the side and from behind. Each requires a slightly different method.

*TACKLING*
**Far left:** *Drive hard into the ball-carrier*
**Left:** *Head behind and legs bent for drive*
**Above:** *Drive through to put the ball-carrier off balance*

## Front tackling
## (sometimes called head-on tackling)

There are two separate types of this tackle: the passive and the blockbuster. The first is when the tackler allows the ball-carrier to approach and then brings him down using the carrier's momentum to complete the tackle. Remember to position your head, allow the carrier virtually to run into you, drop your tackling shoulder and encircle his thighs. Once your grip is complete with your shoulder blocking his progress, apply pressure so that the attacker's own weight forces him to fall sideways.

In the blockbuster the target area for the tackler is the waist. The success of this tackle depends on your anticipation and speed of

*FRONT TACKLING*
**Right:** *The blockbuster tackle*
**Far right:** *The passive tackle*

execution. When you spot the ball-carrier is in the position you have anticipated, move in quickly. Place your head alongside the player, grip under his centre of gravity, i.e. below his buttocks, and then pull and lift at the same time. Drive the ball-carrier back and land on top with your shoulder in the target area.

*REAR TACKLE*
**Right:** *Eyes fixed on target area for rear tackle*
**Far right:** *Grip firmly round ball-carrier's thighs*

## Rear tackle and side tackle

Once a player has broken through it is very likely that you will have to catch and tackle him from behind. Take care to stay away from his boots and use the basic method as described on the previous pages. The side tackle is probably the easiest of the three to perform. Use the basic method and ensure you keep a grip on the carrier until he is well and truly grounded. Each time the target is the thigh.

**SMOTHER TACKLE**
Left: *Pin the ball between yourself and the ball-carrier*
Below: *Drive through until the ball-carrier is grounded*

## Smother tackle

Quite often in Rugby League there is not enough time to set up a proper tackle. When circumstances dictate that the ball-carrier should not be allowed to pass, that is the time to bring the smother tackle into play. Sometimes it is called the upright tackle because you attempt to prevent the player being in a position to release a pass while stopped in a standing position. When the carrier approaches, move forward and pin the ball between yourself and the carrier's body. Your arms should be wrapped round the upper part of the carrier and his arms should be trapped by his side. It is important to realize that this tackle requires determination and timing so that the carrier is eventually forced to the ground.

# KICKING

Although Rugby League is essentially a handling game, kicking is one of the most important and effective skills available to players and their teams. The simple act of kicking the ball forward can save the grind of driving it forward to gain ground, it can be used to score important points and relieve pressure in critical situations.

There are five ways to kick the ball in Rugby League.

## Punt

If you kick the ball from the hands before it touches the ground it is called a punt. Hold the ball with one of its points aiming the way you are going to kick it. Keep your shoulders square with the target, ensure your head is down and that your eyes do not leave the ball until it is kicked. The ball should be held a comfortable distance away from your body and the boot, when it makes contact, should fit into the rounded area of the ball. Keep the toes pointing forward and drive the foot through the ball. Remember that in broken play if you are looking to make ground then the ball must bounce before it goes into touch otherwise your team will have to return to the spot where the kick was made and concede the advantages of sight and feed at a scrum.

Top: *Hand placing for orthodox punt*
Above: *Positioning for drop kick*

PUNT KICK
Above: *Body position ready for punt kick*
Right: *Notice how the ball fits nicely in the arc of the foot*
Far right: *The essential good follow-through*

## Torpedo punt

The second variety of punt kick is called a torpedo. It receives its name because when the ball is kicked it spins through the air like a torpedo or bullet, helping the kicker gain valuable extra distance. To impart the spinning effect you must vary the normal punt technique. It is essential to hold the ball correctly – one hand should be placed marginally forward of the other, just under the ball, and it should be held slightly pointing inwards. This means that when you drop the ball it arrives at an angle across the instep; the kicking foot should also be angled inwards when it makes contact. As distance is the object, you should avoid kicking the ball too high, remembering that the spin causes the ball to curve in the air.

## Grubber kick

This useful little kick sends the ball along the ground in advance of your team. It allows your team-mates to run through with a chance of regaining possession while, at the same time, making life very difficult for the defenders trying to gather it up. Hold the ball as if you were going to pass and guide it along the floor with your foot. Make sure that your body is over the ball and send it off with a stabbing kick with no follow-through.

## Kick-over

Tactically, this is a lofted variant of the grubber kick. Use the same stabbing action to punt the ball over the heads of the defenders. As before, avoid following through to keep the kick short.

## Drop kick

Using the same principles as for the punt, the drop kick requires a slight variation in timing because the ball must hit the ground before contact is made. Take care to select your target area and then switch your attention to the kicking area where the ball will

**DROP KICK**
**Far left:** *For a drop kick, angle the ball down so that it is ready to be kicked*
**Left:** *Keep your balance as you make contact with the ball*
**Right:** *Follow right through the ball*

be dropped. Hold the ball clear of your body in the same way as you did to pass and then adjust it to an angle of around 45 degrees relative to the ground. Try to place the ball near the toe of the non-kicking boot and then, with the lower part of the instep, kick the ball. Keep your head and eyes down all the time, spread your arms to help balance and lean slightly back so that your kick gains sufficient height to clear the crossbar. At a re-start, where the length of the carry is more important, delay the actual kick by a fraction.

## Place kick

In this kick the ball is always played from the ground. It is generally used either to re-start a game or to kick at goal and the action should be tailored to suit the circumstances.

Kicking to start a match or re-start it after a score requires work with a team coach. The delivery of the kick has to be measured so that it meets your forwards who are arriving to challenge the opposition for possession. The kick at goal is a precision kick at a still target which, if successful, brings two valuable points for a conversion or a penalty. Both types of kick carry a lot of responsibility and as many team members as possible should practise and be prepared to take place kicks for their side.

There are two methods for place kicking. The first, and more

**PLACE KICK**
**Below:** *For a traditional place kick, place ball firmly on ground with seam facing target*

**Left:** *Ensure one foot is placed alongside ball*
**Right:** *Keep your eye on the ball*
**Far right:** *Kick through the ball*

*Using the elevated angle requires careful preparation*

*The ball placed on a mound of sand or soil ready for place kick*

*Notice the different angle of the ball for a bullet-style place kick*

traditional, involves kicking with the toe after a straight-on approach to the ball. The other involves kicking with the instep in a style known as 'round-the-corner'.

A common factor in both methods is that the ball is teed up like a golf ball. Many British goal-kickers now prefer to have sand or a plastic tee brought on each time they have an attempt at goal, using the sand or plastic tee to make a mound on which to tee the ball. This method became popular after it had been used for many years in Australia and New Zealand. The traditional British method is to make a hole in the turf and build up a tee from the soil. Both have the same effect: they set the ball up for the kicker.

Kickers have another choice. They can place the ball on the tee in an upright position, or make it lean slightly backwards or use the bullet style, laying the ball on the tee with one end pointing at the target. The bullet method requires great care with lining up and it helps to have a seam running the length of the ball facing in the direction of the target. The kicker has to be very careful that he keeps body, ball and target all in a straight line.

The toe-end kicking method has considerable advantages for the beginner. The target, the boot and the player are in a straight line and that makes aiming easier. It is important that only the toe strikes the ball or there can be no guarantee of direction.

No matter which way the ball is placed the same method of approach to the kick is recommended. Once you have mastered your approach to the ball you can concentrate entirely on accuracy. Tee the ball up so that a central point, no more than 2.5cm (1in) from the bottom of the ball, is visible. This is called the spot. Aim a seam of the ball at the target while you are bending over to place the ball. Ensure that you, the ball and the target are in a straight line. Stand directly behind the ball and then place your non-kicking foot by the side of it. This is the moment for your last visual check to see that everything is in line. Keeping your eye on the ball, look at the spot referred to above. Concentrate on that spot until the ball is kicked. Now you should step back however many steps you want for your run-up; at the end of the run-up you pause, then with a rhythmic run approach the ball. When you arrive at the ball your non-kicking foot should return to its earlier place beside the ball. When your body is directly over the ball, your toe should make contact with the spot. Allow your foot to follow through and spread your arms to provide the necessary balance.

In the 'round-the-corner' method you kick the ball soccer-style using the upper part of the instep. That means you have more of the ball to aim at and you can wear lighter-weight boots. The problem, however, is that the trajectory of the ball is curved and a right-footed kicker on the right-hand side of the field finds it naturally difficult to hit the ball on-target. Some teams solve the problem by having one right- and one left-footed kicker.

Instep-kickers begin with the same method of approach, then after stepping out their run-up take a couple of paces to the right or left so that the run-up, apart from the last couple of strides, is curved. It is important to remember those last two steps because they line the kicker up with the target.

# SCRUMMAGE

*The correct method for scrum-halves to feed a scrummage*

The scrummage is the chief unit skill in Rugby League. While the game is often, and justifiably, criticized for its untidy scrums there is a design to them that is not always visible or appreciated by spectators and television viewers. Increasingly over the last two or three seasons more attention has been given to its potential, as demonstrated by successive Australian and New Zealand touring teams, and it is important to include scrummage technique regularly in coaching and training sessions.

It has been said that front-row forwards play their own private game within the match, and there is some truth in this. The whole point of the scrummage is to decide possession for the next play and, because holding the ball is so important, the skill, strength and determination of the front-row trio are crucial.

These three forwards provide a solid platform by binding their arms round each other and then interlocking heads with the opposing front-row forwards. This creates a clear tunnel into which the scrum-half will feed the ball. The moment the ball enters the tunnel the two hookers strike for it using one of their feet; possession is decided when one succeeds in dragging the ball back into his half of the scrummage. The two second-row forwards bind together with their arms and put their heads into the two gaps between the prop forwards and the hooker. Likewise the loose

*Forwards set for a scrummage. Notice the binding of the arms*

forward places his head between the two second-row forwards.

A useful tactic for the open-side prop is to lift his shoulder on the outside of the scrum so that his hooker can have a clear view of the ball at the feed. This has the effect of giving the scrum a humped appearance but is legal provided the binding between the players is maintained.

Before the put-in the players' bodies should be almost horizontal to the ground from the waist up, and in a pushing position. The scrummage is then ready to receive the ball. The scrum-half whose team has been awarded the put-in re-starts play on the instruction of the referee. Because winning possession at the scrummage is so important, your scrum-half and front-row forwards should regularly practise the put-in procedure using verbal and other signals to indicate when the ball is likely to enter the tunnel. This gives the hooker an advantage over his opposite number because he will know precisely when the feed is going to happen.

As a unit the forwards should be trained to deliver concerted pushes once the ball is fed into the scrum. A good push, linked to a strike by the hooker, is the best way to be sure of winning the ball. Once the hooker has taken the ball it should be channelled between the second-row forwards to the rear of the scrum. After it has gone through the second row the ball is in play and the scrum-half can pick it up.

The scrummage is a physically demanding set-piece and forwards should be fit enough to cope with its pressures. Upper-body strength is clearly an asset, linked to the stamina required to last and be effective for the full 80 minutes of a match.

# TACTICAL USE OF SKILLS

Once players have an understanding of the basic skills they can settle down to enjoy playing the game. Now they are ready to learn the extra individual skills that make a team member into a Rugby player.

## Acceleration
You do not run at a single speed. You can vary your pace to suit every circumstance. For wingers particularly, the injection of sudden extra pace can be devastating. A defender believes that he has you trapped, and then you leave him stranded by accelerating away from him. The ability to vary your pace during a run always makes it more difficult for the defenders.

## Bump-off
This is a skill that will help prevent ball-carriers being successfully tackled. As the defender comes in to make the tackle, the carrier should use a hard part of the body, the shoulder in particular, to bump-off the opponent. When using the chest players should fold their arms over the ball so that the brunt of the collision is taken on the forearm.

*Preparing to bump-off a tackler*

## Swerve

The ball-carrier always has the advantage of knowing what he
wants to achieve and can throw off potential tacklers with the
gentle art of deception. Footwork is the key to a successful swerve,
and timing is critical. Imagine a tackler coming in from the left. At
the last moment you move to the right, balancing on the outside of
your right foot and the inside of the left foot as you run. This takes
you away from the tackler. To swerve left, simply reverse the
balance points.

## Dummy

Every Rugby player in the world at some stage in his career has
bought, as they say, a dummy. That means they have been left
stranded by another player who has fooled them into thinking he
was going to pass and then did not.

The player in possession holds the ball out as if he was going
to pass to a team-mate. He goes through the motions of passing
and then, at the last possible moment, holds on to the ball. The
secret of selling a dummy is to catch the eye of the defender. He
sees you setting up the pass and then sets off in pursuit of where
he thinks the ball has gone.

*A well-placed hand-off can prevent a successful tackle*

## Hand-off

This is called the fend- or palm-off in Australia and is used by ball-carriers when they are attempting to keep a tackling player at bay. The carrier switches the ball to one hand and pushes the defender off with the other. It should not be executed too early or the tackler will be able to take avoiding action. You should aim the palm of your hand – not your fist, that is foul play – towards your opponent's forehead, chest or shoulder and then deliver a firm push.

## Side-step

If you are advancing as a ball-carrier straight at a tackler who is bent down and in position to tackle you one of the best ways of beating him is by side-stepping. As you arrive within the tackler's range simply drive your left foot into the turf with all your weight on your toes. This brings your speed down dramatically and allows you to switch your weight to the right. To side-step left, reverse the pattern.

Then take a long stride to the right. The moment the right foot touches the ground push on it and take your left leg straight through, continuing your run. You should develop the skill so that you can side-step in both directions. If you can only go one way other players will be able to anticipate your ploy. When executed properly the side-step leaves tacklers groping at shadows.

## Extra man and overlap

When you are playing against a team who can tackle well you have to create scoring chances either by penetrating their line with some of the running ploys we have just described or by outflanking them. If you merely pass the ball along the line to the winger the movement will break down when he is tackled by his opposite number. If, however, your full-back forsakes his defensive role and joins the three-quarter line as they attack there will be an extra attacker available at the end who can beat the defence.

The overlap can also be achieved by one player such as a centre three-quarter pulling one or two opposing three-quarters out of position by forcing them to tackle him and then passing the ball to a team-mate.

## Support play

In Rugby League you can never hope to beat every tackle in every game. On many occasions it is to your team's advantage if you take the tackle and, before you are grounded, pass to a player coming in behind you. It is very little use if, every time you get the ball, you just charge forward into the tacklers. If you drive forward with several of your team-mates following it means that even if you are stopped, the movement can continue if you pass the ball. A general rule for all League players is: 'Support the ball-carrier'. You can never tell when a defensive error or scoring chance is going to happen.

## Kick ahead

Against a defensive line that is lying flat, marking the attacking side man-for-man, a short kick ahead can break through the line and give the advancing attackers a chance to continue pressing home their advance. A cross-field kick behind the defenders to your wing, especially when used with a pre-arranged signal, can be very effective because it turns the defence and has them running back towards their line.

*A reverse pass can fool your opposition*

## Reverse pass

In Rugby League it is often an advantage to switch the direction of play at the last possible second, and a most important part of that operation is the reverse pass. It can be performed in two distinct ways. First, the passer can turn his body virtually to face his own goal-line and look at the receiver who will move inside and behind him. The ball is then simply transferred in the usual way in the direction of the receiver's run, and the advantage of this method is that the passer never loses sight of the player to whom he is giving the ball.

The second is a more complicated method which requires a great deal of understanding between team-mates. The passer continues upfield towards the opponent's try-line and, as he runs, slips the ball up and behind him ensuring that he runs in front of the receiver. The receiver collects the ball at the last possible second and changes the direction of the attack.

These more sophisticated methods of passing add considerable variety to a team's tactical approach to the game.

## Scissors

As one player moves diagonally across the field in one direction he passes the ball to a team-mate going in the opposite direction. This works best if the delivery can be disguised until the last moment and the ball is 'smuggled' away. As with all passing moves, the more you practise the better you play.

*Timing is essential in a scissors movement*

## Up-and-under or bomb kick

When you reach the fifth tackle and are close to your opponents'
line, one of the best ways to create a scoring chance is to loft a very
high punt. It puts considerable pressure on the defenders who may
then make a mistake and concede possession.

There is no advantage in kicking directly into the in-goal area
around the goal-posts because if the full-back catches the ball
cleanly he can re-start the game in possession with a 22-metre tap
kick. Some professionals have found that they gain more by kicking
across the field of play.

# POSITIONAL PLAY

One of the most important terms you are likely to hear in modern
Rugby League is 'game-plan'. Basically it refers to the plan of
campaign your coach has devised before the match. This means that
your game becomes easier to organize on the field of play because
you know your team and individual targets. Of course, plans can
change and there is always room for individual flair, but as playing
standards rise the need for pre-planning becomes more necessary.

In Rugby League, the players' positions remain the same
wherever the game is played. A country may change the name it
gives to a position or move but the essence of each player's job
remains identical. This means a firm definition and responsibility

*The full-back has many attacking options and can cover all the gaps in the defensive line*

can be given to each position. It is important that these roles are understood by the whole team because a successful outfit depends on each player knowing what is required of him and how his role fits in with those of his team-mates. Understandably too, every team member wants to think that he can rely on everyone else once the action starts.

## Full-back

He is the last line of defence and can also be the first of attack. The full-back stands at the rear of the team and must be both a sure handler of the ball and a sound tackler. In modern Rugby League the high kick deep into the opponents' half is used frequently to seek out weak points and force defensive errors. In defence the full-back has to be a confident catcher and be able to gather the ball safely from the ground. When he is called upon to tackle it is usually in critical circumstances and he must be proficient at taking players to the ground or preventing them from passing.

That is one half of the full-back's role. Because he plays so deep in the defence he has a great overall view of the game and can judge the perfect moment to link up with his three-quarter line as the extra man in attack or to pick the ideal spot for a penetrating kick into the opposition half. For that reason many of the top full-backs in Rugby League tend to be very proficient kickers.

## Wing three-quarter

There are two wingers in each team, left and right. It is a highly individualistic role. Their main function is to use speed and strength to score tries and they are also expected to add tackling support when the situation demands, for example in covering across if an opponent breaks away. Each wing has his own way of doing his job but, in general, there are two varieties of winger. One, usually a player with extra speed, will try to create space and time with elusive running, calling on side-steps, swerves and dummies while the second, usually a more robust type of player, will employ straight, powerful running with changes of pace and bump-offs in his path to the goal-line.

## Centre three-quarter

The centre occupies one of the most interesting attacking positions on the team. He carries great responsibility and as part of the team's main attacking machinery he has a two-fold role.

He can either utilize his own individual skills and score himself or create dangerous situations that draw defenders in to meet him thereby creating space on the outside for a well-timed pass to reach an unmarked winger. The position is usually given to players who read the game well, and have pace and strength. Because most of their play is carried out at speed, centres should possess a good understanding with each other and with their wing men and stand-off half. Some teams prefer to operate a system where the same centre operates next to the stand-off half all through the game; he is generally known as the inside centre and his partner is the outside centre. More often, however, centres operate at left and right covering zones of the pitch. Good tackling ability is essential for centres who must resist the many attacking thrusts aimed through the middle of the three-quarter line.

## Stand-off half

The stand-off must have great tactical awareness. He controls the ball supply to the backs and on his shoulders rests the decision when and how to attack through the three-quarters. He should also be able to take the initiative himself and for this he needs speed off the mark as well as tactical knowlege. He should be adept at evasive running and have good handling skills. This is one of the most demanding roles in the game and it is not surprising that a great stand-off can have an enormous impact on the game.

## Scrum-half

More often than not the scrum-half is the smallest man on the team. He is selected for his agility and dexterity while, at the same time, he has to be extremely durable because of the number of tackles he has to perform and absorb. It is a position where individual skills count a great deal and he has tremendous impact on the game as a whole.

His main role is to act as a liaison between the forwards and the rest of the backs. He usually sees more of the ball than any other player in the team and, because of that, takes more responsibility. He can spoil a game-plan by holding on to the ball and attempting too much on his own. His main job is to provide the three-quarters with a fast, efficient service from behind the scrum.

The forwards' role in the scrummage has already been discussed but their contribution to the game goes far beyond that. They play a hugely important part in open play and their command of their positional jobs is of utmost importance to the team.

## Loose or lock forward

Like the Queen in chess, the loose forward is a very versatile player. He is usually the first player away from a scrummage and has to provide solid support for the scrum-half and the rest of the back division. It is an advantage if the loose forward has good pace because he is often used as one of the main runners through the gaps that appear in defence on either the open or blind side of a scrummage.

At the base of the scrum he works in tandem with the scrum-half, releasing possession after a scrum when he believes the moment is right for his half-back and acts as a defensive screen to prevent defenders reaching the scrum-half. In defence he should constantly cover the player in possession, and this requires high levels of fitness and mobility.

## Second-row forward

The second-row forwards are beasts of burden and the term 'engine room of the team' describes them perfectly. They are usually highly mobile players who spend a great deal of time carrying the ball at the opposition and tackling. At play-the-ball situations it is often the second-row men who are called upon to run at first man off the acting half-back as well as making themselves available in broken play to carry the ball as far as possible. One of the most useful assets of a second-row forward is a talent for backing up, and that means being constantly available to any player in possession, ready in case they are tackled and want to pass. Defensively, a second-row has to be constantly involved and his tackle-count at the end of the match should be among the highest recorded.

## Prop forward

Physically, prop forwards need to be among the largest members of the side. Their role in the scrum requires power, and they play important roles in the attacking and defensive effort outside the set pieces. Many prop forwards combine their power with a great ball-handling skill to compensate for their lack of blistering pace. They can create openings for other players by taking the tackles and holding off the moment when they are brought down long enough to release the ball to a player who is free to continue the attack.

Props share the general duties of driving the ball upfield and supporting other players. The blind-side prop usually makes a big contribution to the tackle workload. Some props possess pace and can be devastating on a wild run while others are excellent goal-kickers. In a sharp burst, most props can create large holes in a defence if their runs are timed well off short-range passes.

## Hooker

Once he is released from his scrummaging duties the hooker is now expected to add considerably to both attack and defence. In the past he trundled from scrum to scrum and, as long as he won the ball, that was all that was required of him. Today, he is a versatile player, often used as the acting half-back. Some modern hookers are super-mobile players who can dictate the pattern of play after a play-the-ball. In addition, of course, he has to share the more everyday ball-carrying and tackling duties with the rest of the pack.

# Useful
# addresses

**Super League America**
112 Stanley Court
Aston
Pa 19014, USA

**Australian Rugby Football League**
Fifth Floor
165 Phillip Street
Sydney
2000 NSW, Australia

**Australian Super League**
Level Ten
287 Elizabeth Street
Sydney
2000 NSW, Australia

**British Amateur Rugby League
Association**
West Yorkshire House
4 New North Parade
Huddersfield HD1 5JP

**Canadian Rugby League**
PO Box 16086
Station 'F'
Ottawa, Ontario
Canada K2C 3S9

**Cook Islands Rugby League**
PO Box 455
Avarua, Raratonga
Cook Islands, South West Pacific

**Fédération de Rugby à Treize**
30 Rue de L'Echiquier
75010 Paris
France

**Fijian Rugby League**
22 Cumming Street
Suva, Fiji

**Moldovan Rugby League**
c/o Gagarina Boulevard 1, Apt 15
27800 Tiraspol, Moldova

**Moroccan Rugby League**
Rue 170, No 103
Hay Oulfa, Groupe H
Casablanca 02
Morocco

**New Zealand Rugby Football League**
CPO Box 712
Auckland 1
New Zealand

**Papua New Guinea Rugby Football
League**
PO Box 1095
Boroko, Papua New Guinea

**Rugby Football League**
Red Hall
Red Hall Lane
Leeds LS17 8NB

**Russian Rugby League**
14 Chapaevsky Per
Moscow 125252
Russia

**South African Rugby League**
22 Tierout Street
Freeway Park
Boksburg 1459
Gauteng, South Africa

**Student Rugby League**
Room 4 Block D
Bishop's Court
Hopwood Hall College
Rochdale Road
Middleton
Manchester M24 6XH

**Tonga Rugby League**
Parliament House
Nuku'alofa
Kingdom of Tonga

**Western Samoan Rugby League**
PO Box 3281
Apia
Western Samoa

# Rules clinic

# index

Figures in *italics* indicate illustrations

# index

Figures in *italics* indicate illustrations

A Ward Lock Book • Cassell • Wellington House • 125 Strand • London WC2R 0BB

A Cassell Imprint • Copyright © Ward Lock 1998

Distributed in the United States by • Sterling Publishing Co. Inc. • 387 Park Avenue South • New York NY 10016 • USA

British Library Cataloguing-in-Publication Data • A catalogue record for this book is available from the British Library

ISBN 0-7063-7712-5

Designed by Grahame Dudley Associates • Illustrations by Pond & Giles • Text revisions by John Huxley

Printed and bound in Spain by Graficromo S.A., Cordoba